Contents

Strange but True 1
Ganges River Dolphin 6
Slow Loris 10
Sri Lanka Frogmouth 14
Clownfish 18
Great Indian Hornbill 22
Hagfish 26
Indian Pangolin 30
Coconut Crab 34
Jewel Wasp 38
Lammergeier.................................. 42
Spot Them Here! 46
Fact Finder and Credits 47

Strange but True

Why do you suppose some animals have incredible abilities? Animals develop these unique qualities so they can live and survive in the different habitats they call home. Evolution – the process by which living things can gradually change over time – has armed animals with superpowers of survival.

These traits are not accidental. They are the product of nature's smart design to help animals find food, escape danger and survive tough environments. Take a look around – you might spot some of these unusual abilities closer to home than you'd expect!

Coral reefs in Indian waters are home to the clownfish

Neighbourhood Oddities

Imagine having the ability to disappear in plain sight! The Indian leaf butterfly is a perfect hide-and-seek artist, rolling its wings up to resemble a shrivelled-up leaf and making itself nearly invisible. The common raven – the crow's larger cousin – can fly upside down. Sometimes, they do it just for fun, but they also use this ability to slow down and lose height as they fly.

The Indian leaf butterfly, found in the Himalayas and central India

What Tricks Do Our Pets Have up Their Sleeves?

Even our pets have astounding secret gifts. Dogs, for instance, have a highly developed sense of smell that allows them to follow scents and discover treasures that the human eye cannot spot. Have you ever seen a cat leap from a great height and land on its feet? Well, this is thanks to their flexible spines and keen sense of balance. This unique ability is called the "righting reflex", which helps them survive falls.

What Makes Humans Special?

Have you ever wondered why we have two legs, while most other animals have four legs? Bipedalism, or walking and standing on two legs, frees up our hands for other tasks, like writing. Opposable thumbs and well-developed brains are some of our other special traits. These have helped humans communicate, grow their food, hunt, create beautiful works of art, develop technology and build large civilizations.

Early humans evolved to walk upright and learnt to hunt

Ganges River Dolphin

Find Me Here!

In the Ganges, Brahmaputra and their tributaries in Uttar Pradesh, Bihar, Assam and West Bengal.

CRITTER STATS

Scientific name: *Platanista gangetica*
Size: 2–2.6 m – as long as a regular bed
Weight: 70–90 kg
Lifespan: up to 30 years
Habitat: freshwater rivers
Conservation status: endangered

With its cheeky smile and inquisitive nature, the Ganges river dolphin is an adorable creature that can be found – you guessed it – in the waters of the Ganges river. While it is known for its playful nature, what sets it apart from other swimmers is its ability to swim sideways.

Being a sideways swimmer is great for hunting in the murky waters of the Ganges.

The Ganges river dolphin can flip onto one side so that its flippers trail along the bottom of the river.

This unique behaviour helps it use its flippers to stir up the muddy riverbed, flushing out hidden prey like fish, crabs and shrimp.

As the prey are driven out of their hiding spots, the dolphin's long, slender snout makes quick business of catching the slippery fish and shrimp.

The dolphin must then head back to the surface because it cannot breathe underwater indefinitely.

All this action takes place in a matter of just 30 seconds to 2 minutes!

DID YOU KNOW?

The Ganges river dolphin makes a peculiar sound while breathing. Thanks to this sound, it is also called "susu" in parts of India.

This river dolphin is nearly blind. It "sees" with sound by using sound waves and echoes to figure out the location of an object.

Slow Loris

Find Me Here!

Lives in the dense forests of Northeast India. Can be spotted at Kaziranga National Park.

CRITTER STATS
Scientific name: *Nycticebus bengalensis*
Size: 26–38 cm – like a loaf of bread
Weight: 0.6–2.1 kg
Lifespan: 20 years
Habitat: evergreen and semi-evergreen forests
Conservation status: vulnerable

Found deep inside the tropical jungles of Northeast India, the slow loris is a nocturnal creature that sleeps during the day and hunts at night. It spends most of its life in the treetops and rarely comes down.

The slow loris moves painfully slowly (just 1.5 km in an hour) and can sit on a branch for hours.

Its hands and feet have adapted to this slow tree life and can grip branches for extended periods of time.

Special glands in the loris's elbows produce a frightfully stinky, oily secretion. When threatened, the slow loris discreetly licks its elbows, mixing the toxin with its saliva.

This little animal also has a secret superpower – it is one of the very few venomous mammals in the world!

A bite from a slow loris can cause severe pain and even make flesh rot!

DID YOU KNOW?

The slow loris feeds on gum and sap found in trees like beech and goomar teak.

Its bottom teeth have a "toothcomb" structure that allows it to scrape gum from the bark of trees.

The slow loris has two tongues: one to slurp nectar and a second to clean the toothcomb!

Sri Lanka Frogmouth

Find Me Here!

Camouflaged in the jungles of the Western Ghats, across Kerala, Tamil Nadu, Karnataka and parts of Goa!

CRITTER STATS

Scientific name: *Batrachostomus moniliger*
Size: 23 cm – about the size of a pigeon
Weight: about 50 g
Lifespan: 5–7 years
Habitat: dense wet forests
Conservation status: least concern

A master of disguise, the wily Sri Lanka frogmouth has feathers that blend seamlessly with the forest. This bird is called the frogmouth after its wide, frog-like mouth.

The Sri Lanka frogmouth is a nocturnal bird.

It comes alive at night, when it catches tasty little insects in its enormous mouth.

During the day, it remains perfectly still, disappearing among the twigs and leaves around it. Its brown and grey feathers make it nearly invisible to predators and curious eyes.

This superpower comes in handy when it's time to hatch eggs. Unlike most birds, it doesn't build a typical nest.

Instead, it lays its eggs on a simple platform made of twigs, relying on its camouflage to protect its young.

DID YOU KNOW?

The Sri Lanka frogmouth can be recognized by its haunting, low-pitched calls of "kro-kro-kro".

Frogmouths often mate for life and are spotted in pairs, roosting quietly on branches.

They lay just one egg! Both parents take turns to sit on the eggs until they hatch. The male takes care of the nest during the day and the female at night.

Clownfish

Find Me Here!

Hiding among the sea anemones and the coral reefs near the Gulf of Mannar and the Andaman and Nicobar Islands!

CRITTER STATS
Scientific name: *Amphiprion sebae*
Size: 8–11 cm – like a toothbrush
Weight: about 0.2 kg
Lifespan: 6–10 years
Habitat: coral reefs with anemones
Conservation status: least concern

You might have seen the brightly coloured clownfish in *Finding Nemo*. Well, you can find the real deal in the coral reefs and warm waters of the Indian and Pacific Oceans. These fish are social butterflies that live in groups of male fish that are led by a female.

This fish, with its bright orange and white stripes, also has a remarkable secret that makes it one of the ocean's most fascinating residents.

In a group, the largest and strongest fish is always female, while the second-in-command is a male. But all clownfish are born male!

If the female leader of a group dies or is removed, the dominant male undergoes a truly mind-boggling transformation, changing into a female to take her place.

This ability ensures that there is always a pair of parents ready to give birth to the next generation of clownfish.

DID YOU KNOW?

Clownfish communicate with each other through popping and clicking sounds.

The gender switch happens only once. When a male turns into a female, she cannot switch back.

Once eggs are laid, the male clownfish guards them until they hatch. He also takes care of the young fish.

Great Indian Hornbill

Find Me Here!

Soars above forests in Uttarakhand, Northeast India and the Western Ghats.

CRITTER STATS

Scientific name: *Buceros bicornis*
Wingspan: up to 150 cm – like a large dog
Weight: 2.2–4 kg
Lifespan: 35–50 years
Habitat: tropical forests with large nesting trees
Conservation status: vulnerable

The first thing you notice about the great Indian hornbill is its large, colourful beak topped by a casque (a hollow, bulging helmet-like structure). And if you don't spot their beaks first, the bird's striking yellow, black and white feathers make it truly hard to miss!

But these birds are not just beautiful – they are also some of the most dedicated parents in the animal kingdom.

Hornbills pairs stay together for life and bring up baby hornbills together year after year. When it's time to lay eggs, the female hornbill seals herself inside a tree.

She does this by using mud, droppings and food, leaving only a small slit open. This slit is just big enough for the male to pass food through. And that he does, day after day.

This remarkable teamwork ensures the baby hornbills stay healthy and safe. Talk about dedication!

 DID YOU KNOW?

Farmers of the forest, they poop out seeds of fruits all over the forest. Some of these grow into new trees!

The hornbill's casque is not just for show – it helps amplify their calls, spreading echoes through the forest.

You can hear the wingbeat of a hornbill from nearly a kilometre away.

Hagfish

Find Me Here!
Found in deep seawater along the Indian coast, especially off Kerala and Tamil Nadu.

CRITTER STATS

Family: *Eptatretus goliath*
Size: 40–80 cm – like a rolling pin!
Weight: about 1–1.6 kg
Lifespan: 30–40 years
Habitat: waters near the muddy ocean floor
Conservation status: not evaluated

In the depths of the Indian Ocean lurks the hagfish, a creature whose mouth makes it look like an alien (the badass kind). This looker of a fish has remained unchanged for 300 million years, making it a living fossil.

But what really sets this creature apart is its incredible ability to produce slime – lots and lots of it!

This one-stop slime factory can secrete copious amounts of the oozy stuff – enough to fill a whole bucket – in just a matter of minutes.

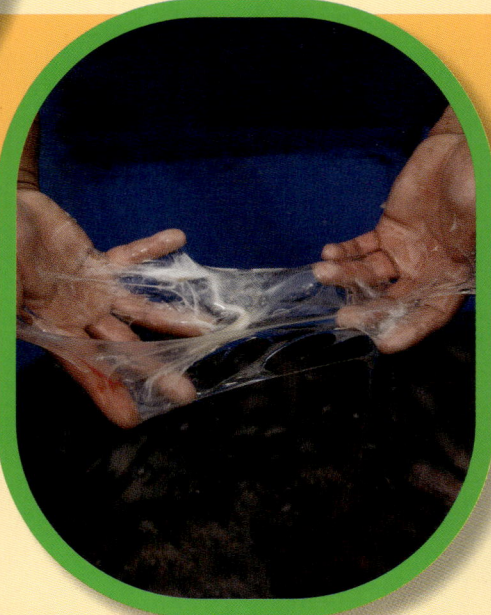

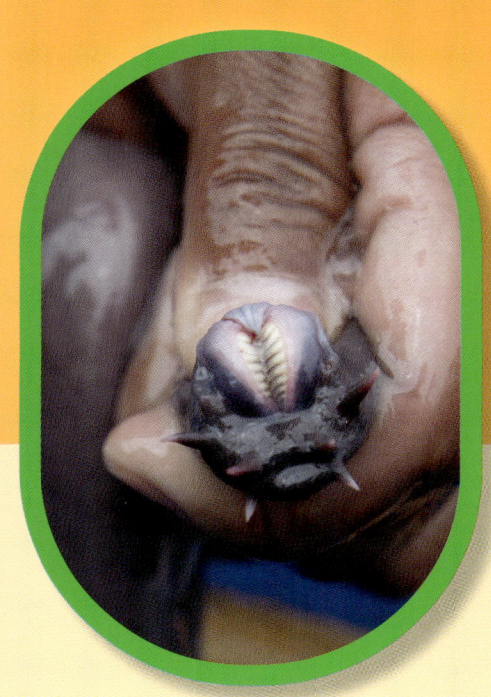

Its body is covered in special glands that give out a mucus-like substance, which expands rapidly in water.

When threatened, the hagfish releases this gooey substance, clogging the gills of predators trying to eat it, allowing it to literally "slip" away.

Hagfish keep the ocean floor tidy by feeding on decaying matter.

 DID YOU KNOW?

Hagfish can tie themselves in knots and slide the knots up and down their bodies to remove excess slime.

They have four hearts that can continue to beat for 36 hours without any oxygen at all! This fish can also survive for months without food.

Hagfish have unusual eating habits. They slide into dead or dying fish and eat them from the inside out. Not a dinner party for the faint of heart!

Indian Pangolin

Find Me Here! Best seen in the scrublands of Madhya Pradesh, Maharashtra and Tamil Nadu, though they live across India.

CRITTER STATS

Family: *Manis crassicaudata*
Size: 60–90 cm – like a cricket bat
Weight: 10–16 kg
Lifespan: 12–20 years
Habitat: scrub, burrows and dry grassy land
Conservation status: endangered

The pangolin roams across much of India, except the desert areas, and the far north-eastern and high Himalayan regions. Tough, overlapping scales cover the pangolin's body, making it the animal kingdom's knight in armour.

The scales are made of keratin – the same stuff that your nails are made of!

When threatened, the pangolin curls up into a tight ball, using its scales as a shield against predators.

The pangolin's tail is covered in even sharper scales. When it lashes it out in defence, these scales can slice through a predator's skin. Ouch!

Also called the scaly anteater, the pangolin is known for its incredible appetite for ants and termites, consuming up to 70 million of these insects each year.

With its long, sticky tongue – which can be longer than its body – the pangolin can reach deep into anthills and termite mounds. This is really important for our planet as it controls insect populations.

DID YOU KNOW?

Pangolins are the only mammals completely covered in scales.

Sadly, pangolins are the most trafficked mammals in the world, making conservation efforts crucial.

They have no teeth. Instead they eat little rocks and stones that sit in their stomachs and help grind up the insects they eat.

Coconut Crab

Find Me Here!
Catch this rare sight near beaches and on coconut trees lining the forests of the Andaman and Nicobar Islands.

CRITTER STATS
Family: *Birgus latro*
Length: up to 40 cm – like a car's steering wheel
Weight: up to 4 kg
Lifespan: 40–60 years
Habitat: coastal forests and rocky crevices
Conservation status: vulnerable

The coconut crab, the largest land crab, can be found burrowing into soil and rocky crevices along coastal forests. This enormous creature can lift up to 30 kg, scale coconut and palm trees and crack coconuts open with ease!

Coconut crabs have claw-like walking legs that curve inwards. This is what helps them to grip tree trunks – even those as straight as the coconut tree's!

They climb up huge trees, grab the coconuts and drop them to the ground.

Then it's time for a leisurely treat. Once they have a coconut in their grasp, they use their super strong claws to crack open the hard shell to feast on the soft flesh inside.

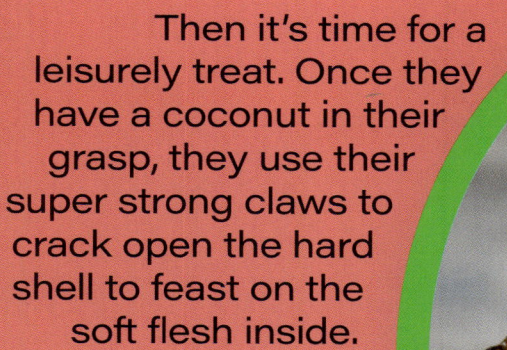

When they're not busy munching coconuts, these crabs can be found feasting on fruits, small animals like rats and sea birds.

DID YOU KNOW?

Coconut crabs are also called robber crabs for their habit of pinching items from unsuspecting picnickers!

A nocturnal animal that forages in the dark, this crab has a remarkable sense of smell that helps them locate food from great distances.

Live life king-size! A female crab lays up to 200,000 eggs in the ocean at one go! These massive crabs begin their lives as miniscule larvae.

Jewel Wasp

Find Me Here!

Found in the gardens and forests in warm, humid areas, often near cockroach habitats.

CRITTER STATS

Family: *Ampulex compressa*
Length: 2.2 cm – like a matchstick
Weight: <0.01 kg
Lifespan: few months
Habitat: warm areas with insect prey nearby
Conservation status: not evaluated

The stunning jewel wasp is a truly dazzling creature with a shimmering emerald body. But don't let its beauty distract you – this wasp has mind controlling abilities! When it's time to lay eggs, the female wasp sets of on a mission to find a nice big cockroach to be her host.

Once she has made her pick, she delivers a two-part sting. The first sting paralyses the roach's front legs temporarily.

The second sting is the real magic. It targets the roach's brain with precision, specifically the part that controls its escape reflex.

This sting doesn't kill the cockroach but instead turns it into a zombie, unable to escape. Hungry after all this stinging, the wasp then chews off half of the roach's antennae to restore its energy.

Finally, using the stubs of the antennae like a leash, it leads the zombi-fied roach back to her nest. Here, she lays an egg on the roach and seals the entrance.

As the larva grows, it eats the still-living roach, before emerging as a new wasp.

 DID YOU KNOW?

The jewel wasp larvae demand the freshest food. Once hatched, they munch on the cockroach parts in a specific order, beginning with non-essential organs to keep the host roach alive for as long as possible.

Despite their fearsome reputation, these wasps are harmless to humans.

Lammergeier

Find Me Here!

The high crags and cliffs of Ladakh, Himachal Pradesh, Uttarakhand, Sikkim and Arunachal Pradesh.

CRITTER STATS

Family: *Gypaetus barbatus*
Wingspan: up to 280 cm – like a king-size bed
Weight: 4.5–7 kg
Lifespan: 20–45 years
Habitat: cliffs, meadows and mountain ridges
Conservation status: near threatened

A bird with a massive wingspan, fiery red eyes and golden plumage, the lammergeier is a legend in the mountains of India. It is also known as the "bearded vulture" for the tufts of feathers under its chin.

But it's not these striking looks that set it apart from the rest. What makes the lammergeier so unusual is its diet – this bird loves bones!

Unlike other vultures, this skeleton-eating bird feeds on bone marrow rather than the meat of its prey. Good choice as the marrow is packed with nutrients!

To find this nutritious treat, the vulture carries large bones high into the air and drops them onto rocks below, shattering them into bite-sized pieces.

This clever technique, known as "ossifrage", allows the lammergeier to thrive in environments where other food sources are scarce.

It can digest the toughest of bones, making it a vital part of the ecosystem.

DID YOU KNOW?

The lammergeier's stomach acid is extremley potent – enough to even dissolve bones!

With a wingspan of up to 9 feet (2.7 m), the lammergeier can glide effortlessly for hours.

The red colour of their feathers is the result of rubbing against damp red soil or bathing in rusty water.

Spot Them Here!

Follow the pug marks to find some of the best places to spot India's amazing wildlife. Creatures like the beautiful jewel wasp live across many regions and can be spotted quite close to home too!

Fact Finder

"Ganges River Dolphin." *WWF*, www.worldwildlife.org/species/ganges-river-dolphin.

"Ganges River Dolphin." *Wildlife Institute of India*, wii.gov.in/nmcg/priority-species/mammals/ganges-river-dolphin.

"The Little Fireface Project: Slow Loris Venom." *Little Fireface Project*, www.nocturama.org/en/slow-loris-venom.

"Slow Loris." *National Geographic*, www.nationalgeographic.com/animals/mammals/facts/slow-loris.

"Sri Lanka Frogmouth." *BirdLife International*, www.birdlife.org/datazone/speciesfactsheet.php?id=2347.

Cornell Lab of Ornithology. "Sri Lanka Frogmouth." *All About Birds*, www.allaboutbirds.org/guide/Sri_Lanka_Frogmouth.

"Great Indian Hornbill." *BirdLife International*, www.birdlife.org/datazone/speciesfactsheet.php?id=963.

"Great Hornbill." National Geographic, www.nationalgeographic.com/animals/birds/facts/great-hornbill.

"Clownfish." *National Geographic*, www.nationalgeographic.com/animals/fish/facts/clownfish.

"Clownfish: The Real Nemo." *Ocean Conservancy*, oceanconservancy.org/blog/2019/06/07/clownfish-real-nemo.

"Hagfish." *National Geographic*, www.nationalgeographic.com/animals/fish/facts/hagfish.

"Hagfish in Indian Waters." *Marine Life of India*, www.marinelifeofindia.org/hagfish.World Wildlife Fund.

"Pangolins." *WWF*, www.worldwildlife.org/species/pangolin.

"Indian Pangolin." *Wildlife Institute of India*, www.wii.gov.in/indian_pangolin.

"Coconut Crab." *National Geographic*, www.nationalgeographic.com/animals/invertebrates/facts/coconut-crab.

"Coconut Crab in India." *Wildlife Institute of India*, www.wii.gov.in/coconut_crab.

"Mind-Controlling Jewel Wasp." *Science Daily*, www.sciencedaily.com/releases/2018/07/180712123456.htm.

"How the Jewel Wasp Turns Cockroaches Into Zombies." *Smithsonian Magazine*, www.smithsonianmag.com/science-nature/how-jewel-wasp-turns-cockroaches-zombies-180960201/.

"Lammergeier." *BirdLife International*, www.birdlife.org/datazone/speciesfactsheet.

"Bearded Vulture." *The Peregrine Fund*, www.peregrinefund.org/explore-raptors-species/BeardedVulture.

Credits

Designer: Abhishikta Dutta

iStockphoto: KristinaPerlerius, #470096059; claudio.arnese, #1068261184; kamui29, #531711852; StuPorts, #140071753; RichLindie, #1222025430; StuPorts, #166281634; Banu R, #1468246970; Marvin Samuel Tolentino Pineda, #1397299930; Banu R, #1468247006; maximilian-nils, #2205991817; cookelma, #2192263944; eli77, #487074633; Joppi, #1133170369; Andyworks, #672768678; slowmotiongli, #1254527684; SeppFriedhuber, #180736884; Luftaufnahme Bayern, #2157821565; svehlik, #172450736; svehlik, #490063401; Banu R, #1471410160; Rishi Kadikar, #1465954972; maximilian-nils, #2205993269; Sourabh Bharti, #2177065565; Thinker360, #1420676204; Sourabh Bharti, #1693429102; jbhavya, #537356122; SWAPNIL MEHTA, #1454113473; Karan Mota, #1297665246; aaprophoto, #1286762694; Miropa, #1219566867; Miropa, #1219566876; picture Umar, #2062965782; Martin Leber, #2178857566; guenterguni, #955522976; Banu R, #1407557845; Sourabh Bharti, #1492878037; pjmalsbury, #94973639; Sourabh Bharti, #1070688080; Sourabh Bharti, #1884972665; Banu R, #1441354008; Banu R, #1425117342; Sourabh Bharti, #1279091687; Robert Knofe, #1037573942; guenterguni, #1210401755; Miropa, #1219518963; Miropa, #1219518937; guenterguni, #1210401618; Rellerfl, #1453687914; wrangel, #481084422; Robert Knofe, #1037573922; maximilian-nils, #2205993269; guenterguni, #1210401698; tane-mahuta, #1292605624; Suman Biswas, #1195662392; Suman Biswas, #1195662505; AmitRane1975, #518110788; Rixipix, #1497364651; Sarah_Cheriton, #177434833; Koushik Bhattacharjee, #1266726638; Rufous52, #527882495; Michel VIARD, #1306654731; wrangel, #917624346; CampPhoto, #1092474326; Utopia_88, #629264484; davemhuntphotography, #156528526; wrangel, #623884592; wrangel, #615279814; slowmotiongli, #1226706821.

Independent contirbutors: Great Indian hornbill by Rohit Nameri; Ganges river dolphin by Sumer Rao; great Indian hornbill by Shashank Dalvi; slow loris by Dhritiman Mukherjee.

First published by Juggernaut Books 2025

Text copyright © Juggernaut Books 2025

10 9 8 7 6 5 4 3 2 1

P-ISBN: 9789353455675
E-ISBN: 9789353458553

All rights reserved. No part of this publication may be reproduced, transmitted, or stored in a retrieval system in any form or by any means without the written permission of the publisher.

Printed at Nutech Print Services - India